SCIENCE VS ANIMAL EXTINCTION

by Nick Hunter

raintree

a Capstone company — publishers for children

Raintree is an imprint of Capstone Global Library
Limited, a company incorporated in England and Wales
having its registered office at 264 Banbury Road, Oxford
OX2 7DY – Registered company number: 6695582

www.raintree.co.uk
myorders@raintree.co.uk

Produced for Raintree by Calcium
Edited by Sarah Eason and Amanda Learmonth
Designed by Simon Borrough
Picture research by Rachel Blount
Production by Victoria Fitzgerald
Originated by Capstone Global Library © 2016
Printed and bound in China

ISBN 978 1 4747 1612 3
19 18 17 16 15
10 9 8 7 6 5 4 3 2 1

British Library Cataloguing in Publication Data
A full catalogue record for this book is available from
the British Library.

Acknowledgements
We would like to thank the following for permission to
reproduce photographs: Dreamstime: Andybignellphoto
19, Coreyford 15, Jilllang 18, Kippis 20, 45br, Kuenzlen
13, 45tc, Maximus117 30, Paulmaguire 12, Petemasty
10, Picstudio 24, Rsfatt 29r, Shootalot 28–29, Smellme
6, Tashka 30–31, Twildlife 21; Shutterstock: Dave Allen
Photography 26, 44–45bg, Ambient Ideas 25, BeauBB
35, Rich Carey 23, 45bl, Darios 41, Evgeny Dubinchuk
22, 45bc, Holbox 34, Idreamphoto 38–39, Wayne Johnson
16, Sebastian Kaulitzski 5, Muriel Lasure 36, LeonP
33, Giancarlo Liguori 43, Maximus256 40, Meirion
Matthias 17, 44b, Steve Oehlenschlager 42, Peteri 8, 44t,
Photostock10 9, PRILL Mediendesign und Fotografie 3,
32, Ratikova 14, 45tr, Dr Ajay Kumar Singh 39b, Sokya
7, Larry St. Pierre 37, Denis Tabler 4, Pal Teravagimov
27, TonyV3112 11.

Cover photographs reproduced with permission of:
Shutterstock: Volodymyr Burdiak (br), Hung Chung
Chih (tl).

Some words are shown in bold, **like this**. You can
find out what they mean by looking in the glossary.

Contents

Our diverse world

Human life is closely linked with the lives of many different **species** of animals. People keep animals, ranging from dogs to snakes, as pets. We also farm animals for their meat, milk and wool. From lions to sharks, we are fascinated by the lives of majestic wild animals. But the animal kingdom is much more complex than it seems on the surface.

Life on Earth
The amazing variety of animal life on Earth is even more remarkable because we know of no other planet that supports animal life.

Earth is the only planet we know that is home to animal life of any kind. This animal life includes large **mammals** such as elephants, lions and humans. It also includes thousands of species of **reptiles**, **amphibians**, birds, fish and **arthropods**, such as insects and spiders. This amazing array of life is called **biodiversity**. It has developed in the 3 billion years since life first appeared on Earth. Scientists have named around 1.8 million different species of living things, including trees and other plants. There are probably millions of species still to be discovered.

ANIMALS UNDER THREAT

The variety of animals and plants on Earth is incredible, but it is also under threat. Throughout Earth's history, species have naturally become **extinct**. But the animal kingdom is now threatened with a disaster because thousands of species may become extinct at once. There are many reasons for this but they share a common factor. The enormous threat to biodiversity comes from one species that is changing Earth beyond recognition – humans.

Under the microscope
Earth's life forms include animals, plants and microorganisms that can only be seen under a microscope.

Winning or losing?
Some scientists believe that in the next 100 years half of all species of life on Earth could become extinct. Science faces a huge challenge to stop this mass extinction from taking place.

Chapter one: Why biodiversity matters

Why does it matter that biodiversity is under threat? After all, we know that animals have become extinct in the past. If there are millions of animal species that have not even been discovered, should we be too concerned if they start dying out?

DEPENDING ON EACH OTHER

Biodiversity matters because no animal can exist without other animals and plants. All the animals and plants in one particular area are called an **ecosystem**. Each member of the ecosystem is essential for the rest of it to thrive. Plants and trees provide food and homes for smaller animals. These smaller animals may be food for larger animals. They may also break down dead animals into nutrients that can be used by plants and trees to help them grow. If something happens to disrupt this system, it can have a dramatic impact on all other animals and plants within it.

Desert landscape
This rocky landscape is a small ecosystem. It is too hot and dry to support a wide range of animals and plants.

In the ring

Charles Darwin (1809–1882) developed the theory of evolution by natural selection when he was a naturalist on a voyage around the world. He discovered a huge range of plant and animal species. His theory stated that animals that were best suited to their environment survived and reproduced successfully. Over millions of years, this survival instinct had created the diversity of life on Earth.

Waste disposal
Insects such as this cockroach do an essential job. They break down dead plant and animal material and return it to the soil.

BIG IMPACT

Many animal species remain undiscovered by humans. Even for those species that we do know about, scientists cannot always find out how they interact with other species in their ecosystem. The loss of any single species could mean that other species lose their main food, without which they cannot survive. If animals start to become extinct at the rate predicted by scientists, this will change ecosystems all over the world. In addition to many animals being lost, there will be a big impact on humans.

Biodiversity and humans

Humans are part of the ecosystems on Earth. People are also fascinated by the vibrant beauty of the animal kingdom. Our lives would be much poorer if animals such as giant pandas and polar bears no longer existed. Yet biodiversity's importance to humans is about more than admiring the wonders of the natural world.

FOOD FOR HUMANS

The lives of people depend on living things, just as much as the lives of other animals do. We grow plants and raise animals for food. Farmers depend on other animals in ways that most of us do not notice, until things start to go wrong.

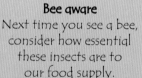

Bee aware
Next time you see a bee, consider how essential these insects are to our food supply.

BEES IN DANGER

In recent years, the number of honeybees has started to shrink in many parts of the world. This directly affects bee-keepers who use the bees to produce honey, but it has a wider impact. Bees play a crucial role in carrying pollen from one plant to another. This enables new plants to grow. More than 90 crops around the world depend on bees. The almond orchards of California are **pollinated** every year by 40 billion bees. With fewer bees, farms that produce our food supplies face serious problems.

HEALTH BENEFITS

Human health depends on biodiversity in other ways. Many of our medicines come from plants. One example is the rosy periwinkle of Madagascar, which contains chemicals that are essential in fighting cancer. There are almost certainly other plant medicines waiting to be discovered. These plants can only thrive if the ecosystems they belong to live remain healthy.

Chapter two:
Animals in crisis

Scientists know that there have been several instances of mass extinction in Earth's history. The last such event happened around 65 million years ago, when a huge **meteorite** collided with Earth. It caused changes in climate and habitats that contributed to the end of the dinosaurs. Surely nothing as catastrophic is happening now?

SEEING DISASTER

Although we may not notice it, the diversity of animal life is under threat as never before. Human activities, such as drilling for and transporting oil, are destroying animal species. If extinctions continue at their current rates, just as the dinosaurs disappeared long ago, we could see entire species wiped out within our lifetimes.

Oil pollution
Pollution from oil spills can have disastrous effects on animals, such as this bird.

HUMANS AND ECOSYSTEMS

Humans' actions lie at the heart of the threat. Habitat loss is just one example. Animal species depend on a particular habitat and the other species within that habitat. Once this habitat is lost or changed, such as by the building of a new motorway, the animals within it cannot survive. Unfortunately, this process speeds up, as the loss of one species means that a number of others do not have enough food.

This is just one of the many ways in which humans affect ecosystems and the animals that live in them. In order to explore how science is fighting back against animal extinction, we need to understand the nature of the threats.

Winning or losing?

Every year, scientists estimate that more than 30,000 species disappear. That is one species every 17 minutes. Many more species that scientists have not yet discovered may be under threat, too. Even if species do not become extinct, they may disappear from a specific location or ecosystem, which, in turn, creates problems for other species.

Destroying habitats

Since humans first started to farm the land, they have cleared forests and grasslands to make way for crops and pastures. Since 1960, the world's human population has more than doubled, and it is continuing to grow. This means that humans need more farmland. More farming causes the loss of wild habitats, but the real problem is that some habitats are more important than others.

TROPICAL RAINFORESTS

Tropical rainforests are our most important ecosystems. These hot, wet forests cover only a small part of the Earth's land, yet they contain a very high proportion of the world's animal and plant species. In some tropical rainforests, 20,000 species of beetle can be found in just 1 hectare (2.5 acres) of land, which is almost as many beetle species as there are in the whole of North America.

The world's largest area of rainforest is in the Amazon River basin of South America. This habitat faces many threats. Logging companies cut down the trees for wood, and mining companies clear the forest in their search for metals and minerals. One of the biggest threats comes from the world's demand for meat, and particularly beef. Large areas of forest have been cut down to make pasture for grazing cattle.

Tropical tragedy
Today, the area covered by tropical rainforest is about half of what it was in the year 1800.

PALM OIL

In the Indonesian rainforest, large numbers of trees have been cleared to make way for palm oil plantations. Orang-utans live in the Indonesian rainforests, and are now under threat because their tree homes have been cut down. Scientists believe this will lead to the extinction of the orang-utan that lives in these forests by 2040.

CORAL CONCERNS

Rainforests are not the only habitats under threat. **Coral** reefs are delicate ecosystems found in tropical oceans. They are under threat too – not because they are a target for farmers but because of **pollution** in the world's oceans.

Turtles and tourists

Turtles are also under threat from tourism. Building hotels can damage the beaches where turtles lay their eggs.

Chemicals and pollution

Pollution takes many forms. Industrial accidents can cause oil or toxic chemicals to spill into delicate environments such as oceans and coastlines. Other forms of pollution occur every day, such as the use of pesticides on crops. Pollution can kill animals that come into contact with it, but it can also affect animals thousands of kilometres away.

THE EFFECT OF OIL SPILLS

The effects of oil spills from tankers or pipelines are clear for all to see. Birds and other sea creatures become coated with the sticky oil. The oil can kill these animals and damage ocean **food chains**. These effects from the oil pollution and also of the chemicals used to clear it up can linger for many years.

Covered by algae
When fertilizers run off fields into water, they cover the surface. This covering stops sunlight from entering the water and encourages algae to bloom. The algae then swamp the water, and nothing else can live there.

Flowing water
Pesticides from farming run into rivers and, eventually, into the oceans. There they harm whales and other sea animals.

PESTICIDE KILLER

The effects of pesticides are more difficult to see. Pesticides are designed to kill insects and other creatures that attack crops. This should mean that fewer crops are spoiled so food is plentiful and inexpensive.

However, when it rains, pesticides are washed off fields into rivers and lakes, where they kill fish. With large numbers of insects killed by pesticides, the food chains of animals that eat insects are also disrupted. Pesticides can remain in the environment for a long time. The pesticide **dichlorodiphenyl-trichloroethane (DDT)** was widely used in the 1950s and 1960s. Even sperm whales, which live in the deep ocean, far from where DDT was used, have traces of the pesticide in their bodies.

In the ring

Marine biologist Rachel Carson (1907–1964) brought the dangers of pesticides to world attention with her book *Silent Spring*. The book explored the impact of the use of the pesticide DDT on songbirds in rural parts of the United States. It led to a worldwide ban of the pesticide.

Introduced species

Until humans started to sail across the oceans, animals on islands or on different continents could evolve without coming into contact with predators from elsewhere. Over time, settlers accidentally carried animals across the oceans on their boats. The introduced animals upset the balance of the new ecosystem.

In the ring

Scientists can accidentally introduce species to a new location. In 2012, scientists working on the deep ocean floor discovered that limpets had attached themselves to their underwater exploration vehicle. These limpets were accidentally transported to another part of the ocean where they could have changed the ecosystem.

Hit by boats

Manatees are harmed when boats sail through their waters and hit them, causing scarring and even death.

Cat attack
Cats can cause big problems in an environment where there were previously no large mammals.

RATS AND CATS

Predators, such as rats and cats, that are common in many places can have a disastrous impact when let loose in areas that have not seen them before. The Stephens Island wren is an example of this. The wren once lived across the islands of New Zealand. This bird could not fly – it had no predators, so did not need to. When rats arrived in the boats of Maori settlers, the flightless wrens were wiped out by the predators on all islands except Stephens Island. When European settlers arrived, the remaining birds were probably killed by the settlers' cat, Tibbles.

TOAD TRAGEDY

Some species are deliberately introduced by humans. The cane toad was taken to Australia from South America to get rid of the cane beetles that attacked sugar crops. The toads then spread out across the country, competing with other toads for food and driving them close to extinction. Cane toads are also poisonous to many animals that eat toads.

Hunting and fishing

Hunting is the most deliberate way in which humans target animals. Some species are highly valued for a particular body part, such as an elephant's tusks. In 2011, the western black rhino was declared extinct. This animal lived in West Africa. The black rhino was made extinct by poachers who killed it for its horn, which was sold for use in Chinese medicine.

Rhino riches
The horn of a black rhino can mean big money to hunters, who are often living in extreme poverty.

Road accident
Even when protected in national parks, moose and deer can be killed by accident in collisions with vehicles.

CLEARING THE OCEANS

Fishing is causing massive damage to the ecosystem of the world's oceans. The oceans are a great source of food, but the 20 million boats catching fish from the sea are threatening ocean biodiversity. Most of these vessels are small fishing boats, but a few of them are huge industrial ships that gather vast numbers of fish and other sea animals. Around 20 per cent of their catch is not fit for sale and is returned to the ocean, often dead. Larger sea animals such as whales and dolphins are often killed when they are caught up in fishing gear.

All of these issues affect the numbers and diversity of life in the oceans. Just as on land, sea animals depend on each other for survival and falling fish numbers are a threat to the food supply of many seabirds.

Winning or losing?

In 2010, a report from the United Nations warned that fish stocks had been reduced by 20 per cent due to overfishing. The report predicted that if this continues, there would be almost no fish left in the sea by 2050. One billion people rely on fish as their main source of essential protein.

Climate change

The biggest threat to biodiversity comes from Earth's changing climate. Scientists have discovered that our climate is getting warmer. This is caused by greenhouse gases, such as carbon dioxide, being released into the **atmosphere** by industry and transport. These gases trap the Sun's energy, causing the climate to warm up.

HABITAT LOSS

Climate change contributes to the loss of important habitats. In the frozen polar regions, warmer climates could completely destroy the habitats of animals such as the polar bear. These animals need ice sheets from which to hunt. Melting ice reduces the length of their hunting season, meaning that the bears cannot catch enough fish to live. Other animals will look for higher ground or move to cooler habitats, and may then disrupt the ecosystems of their new habitats.

Climate change also alters the way living things behave within ecosystems. Scientists are already finding that plants are flowering earlier in the year than they have in the past. Changes such as this will affect many animals because they depend on flowering plants for food.

DESTROYING OUR OCEANS

The oceans absorb much of the carbon dioxide that humans produce. This is making the waters more **acidic**. The change is happening so quickly that ocean plants and animals have little time to adapt to it. Ocean acidification could be even more damaging to sea creatures than overfishing.

Spreading deserts
Climate change will lead to more deserts, where few animals can survive.

No more foxes?
Climate change could destroy habitats for animals such as this Arctic fox, which lives in the icy polar regions.

Winning or losing?
A report in 2012 warned that Earth's climate would become warmer by an average of 3 degrees Celsius (5 degrees Fahrenheit) by 2100 unless urgent action is taken by the world's governments.

Chapter three: Science fights for biodiversity

With so many threats to biodiversity, science has a real fight on its hands to preserve the amazing variety of life on Earth. This fight is not just to protect big mammals, such as rhinos and polar bears, it is also about safeguarding the tiny bugs and plants that are just as important for Earth's ecosystems.

Coral reefs
Amazing coral reefs are important areas of study for scientists as well as homes for the animals that live on them.

In the ring

It is not only scientists who can see the value of biodiversity. Tourists in many of the world,s wildest places come to see the variety of animal life. These tourists bring money to poorer regions of the world and give an incentive for local people to conserve animal life.

Forest fires
Natural disasters, such as forest fires, can damage biodiversity. Science is looking for ways to prevent these disasters.

TIME TO ACT

Scientists' understanding of biodiversity and the threats it faces is increasing all the time. There is no time to waste in taking action to stop the extinction of animal species. Every time a species becomes extinct, it may contribute directly to the loss of further species. Once a species becomes extinct, it is gone forever.

SUCCESS STORIES

Although the news about biodiversity is often bleak, scientists have reported some good news. In 1987, the California condor was close to extinction. The 22 remaining birds were captured and bred in captivity. Once their numbers had recovered sufficiently, some were released into the wild. There are now more than 400 condors on Earth, and around half of these are living in the wild.

For every success story, there is also a story of struggle. For example, New Zealand's kakapo bird is on the brink of extinction as it is unable to deal with introduced predators. If stories such as that of the California condor are to become more common, there are many issues for scientists to tackle.

Measuring biodiversity

The first challenge for scientists is to measure biodiversity. Scientists monitor the number and health of species in different habitats. These measurements are taken to help scientists understand the impact of the various threats to biodiversity.

Measuring biodiversity is more complex than just counting animals that look the same. For example, scientists noticed that some pipistrelle bats made slightly higher pitched calls than others. Investigation of their **deoxyribonucleic acid (DNA)** showed that they were actually different species, even though they looked similar.

WHAT SHOULD WE PROTECT?

Scientists need to decide what to protect. Ecosystems are now so badly damaged that it is too late to save all species. Scientists must look at which habitats and animals will have the biggest impact if lost.

Bat signals
The high-pitched sounds made by bats can be used to tell different bat species apart.

HOW TO PROTECT?

Some larger animals, such as elephants or tigers, can be given special protection, but this is much more difficult with the smaller creatures that are essential in all ecosystems.

One option is to track the number of species in a particular place. With so many species undiscovered, this is not an exact measure. The greatest variety of species on Earth yet to be discovered probably exist in the Earth's rainforests and its deep oceans.

Breaking through

With so many species of animals and plants to be tracked, scientists are searching for ways to make the process easier. Genetic barcodes are one way of doing this. Each product in a supermarket has a different barcode and each species of animal and plant has genetic material or DNA that mark it out as a certain species. Scientists can use this genetic barcode to quickly see if an animal belongs to a species they already know about.

Butterfly counting

Scientists are finding more and more insect species. More than 1,000 species of butterfly were found in just one Peruvian nature reserve.

Protecting habitats

For animals to survive in the wild, habitats must be protected. All habitats contain some animal species, but the most important ecosystems are those that include the biggest variety of species.

NATIONAL PARKS

Thanks to scientists and campaigners, more of the world than ever is protected. National parks are areas where animals and their ecosystems are protected from industry and other threats. The world's biggest national parks include the Amazonia forest reserve in South America. South America is home to much of the world's vital rainforest and also has the most protected land.

National parks
The Great Smoky Mountains National Park in the United States protects many plants and animals.

PROTECTED REEFS

Coral reefs are home to almost as many species as tropical rainforests. The Great Barrier Reef in Australia is a huge protected area. A quarter of all marine species live on coral reefs in warm, tropical seas.

STILL IN DANGER

Some areas are missing out on protection. Vast parts of the world's oceans that are outside the borders of individual countries are largely unprotected. Yet ocean life faces some of the greatest challenges to biodiversity.

Protecting zebras
Zebras are hunted for their skins and meat. Rangers in some national parks are often armed to protect animals from hunters.

ACTIVE PROTECTION

Creating a national park does not just mean leaving nature untouched. Many ecosystems do benefit from human involvement in maintaining different habitats. In other national parks, wardens are literally prepared to fight to protect endangered species that are targets for poachers.

Winning or losing?
In 2011, the clearing of the Brazilian rainforest fell to its lowest level since scientists began to record it, with 6,418 square kilometres (2,477 sq miles) being cleared in that year. But folllowing a change in Brazil's forest protection laws in 2012, forest clearance has since risen sharply.

Restoring habitats

Every year, the number of wilderness areas that could be protected as national parks shrinks. If people restore polluted or damaged habitats, endangered animals will have more space to roam and find food, and a greater chance of avoiding extinction.

MARINE RESTORATION

Chesapeake Bay on the eastern coast of the United States is one region that has tried to restore its marine habitats. Pollution from cities, industries and farming fertilizers and pesticides have polluted the bay. Since the 1980s, states around the bay have reduced pollution and protected wildlife. This restoration was partly to help the local fishing industry. Healthy ecosystems benefit humans as well as animals.

Moving and changing
When people move to new environments, it can badly damage wildlife there. Ecosystems and the food webs within them can be disturbed.

FOREST PROTECTION

Traditional farming methods can help to restore and conserve habitats. Around 250,000 indigenous people live in the Amazon rainforest. These people have relied on the plants and animals of the forest to provide their food and other daily needs for generations. They have cared for the forest for centuries.

WILDLIFE CORRIDORS

Protected areas are often quite small and large animals need space to roam and hunt. Wildlife corridors are large areas of wilderness that link different national parks. They enable animals to move between parks to find food.

In the ring

In 2004, a large team of scientists began a project to compare biodiversity in newly grown forest and tropical rainforest in the same area. They found that many rainforest species were happy to make their homes in new forests that had grown up on abandoned plantations. This gives hope that biodiversity can be restored in the world's damaged ecosystems.

Living together
Indigenous people in rainforests have an interest in protecting the ecosystems they live in.

Cutting pollution

Pollution affects animals in two ways. In the short term, oil spills and pesticides can kill them. In the long term, climate change poses the threat of extinction for millions of animal species. Scientists are fighting hard to protect animal life from the effects of pollution.

Friend or foe?
Biofuels can be used instead of fossil fuels, but growing enough crops to meet energy needs would reduce biodiversity in many areas.

Oil pollution
Fumes from oil refineries are just one reason why scientists are looking for alternatives to fossil fuels.

FUEL FACTOR

The main cause of climate change is the burning of **fossil fuels** such as coal and oil. Scientists are looking for ways to reduce our reliance on these fuels, such as developing nuclear energy production and capturing energy from the Sun. Biofuels are one possible solution. These crops can be used to replace fossil fuels, but many scientists are concerned about their impact on biodiversity. Palm and soya oils used in biofuels are often grown in the tropics, and rainforests may be cut down to make way for the new biofuel crops. Nuclear power was also once considered an alternative fuel supply, but there are now concerns about its safety.

SAFE PESTICIDES?

Pesticides can never be totally harmless, but scientists have made progress towards "safe" pesticides. Organic pesticides are made from natural substances to lessen the impact on the wider environment. In the future, changing plant **genes** to deal with pests could remove the need for pesticides. However, many people think that genetically modified (GM) plants could be more dangerous to ecosystems than pesticides.

Protecting endangered species

Along with measures to protect habitats and cut pollution, scientists must find ways of preserving Earth's rarest species. It is no use protecting the habitats of animals if poachers then kill the animals because their tusks or skins are valuable.

LAWS WORTH BREAKING?

International laws have helped to protect some of the rarest species. There is an international treaty that bans trading in species that scientists have listed as endangered. However, in countries where people live in extreme poverty, the money that can be earned from poaching is so great that people will always attempt to break the law.

Gorilla warfare
Mountain gorillas in central Africa are threatened both by poaching and war, which has affected the area for many years.

SPECIES ON THE EDGE

One way to protect species in danger of dying out is to breed them in captivity. Wild animals can be caught and kept in zoos or protected areas. Once their numbers have started to rise again, they can be released back into the wild. These programmes have become more successful in recent years as scientists have learned more about behaviour in threatened species.

Arabian oryx
The oryx is an example of an animal that has been bred in captivity to increase numbers and then released back into the wild.

Winning or losing?

The International Union for Conservation of Nature (IUCN) produces a list of threatened species. In 2014, there were more than 70,000 animal species on the list, including more than 40 per cent of all amphibians. The number of threatened species increases as new species are found, but there are potentially millions of undiscovered species.

DEADLY DISEASE

Disease can be a major threat to species already dealing with other challenges. As well as habitat loss and climate change, amphibian species have been attacked by a fungus that could threaten their survival. The Amphibian Ark is a group of organizations that have joined together to protect amphibian species threatened with extinction.

Chapter four: Debates and issues

No one wants animals to become extinct. A mass extinction of animal species would cause major problems for humans, and particularly for our food supply. But the threats that animals face are not easy to solve. Scientists and governments do not always agree about the best ways to tackle the problems.

Tuna fishing
You can find tuna in every supermarket, but overfishing means that tuna are now in crisis.

SMALL AND FORGOTTEN

Much of the media coverage of animal extinctions focuses on large animals under threat, such as polar bears and whales. Many conservationists argue that although the loss of these much-loved species would be a tragedy, too much attention is focused on them. The more than one million species of insects, such as the honeybee, are actually more important to the functioning of most ecosystems. They need protection, too.

A GLOBAL PROBLEM

Preserving our Earth's biodiversity needs international cooperation. Even though the tropical rainforests are found close to the equator, humans everywhere benefit from the huge range of species found there. Some countries are simply not able to protect the forests on their own.

The oceans are an even bigger problem as most of the world's seas are beyond the control of individual countries. Overfishing of tuna means that numbers of these fish are declining fast. However, it is difficult to protect tuna because these fish live in international waters, so no one country can be held responsible.

In the ring

Pressure groups campaign to make sure the public and governments know about the crisis facing the world's animals. The World Wildlife Fund (WWF) has been campaigning about conservation issues for more than 50 years. Other organizations focus on specific animals or ecosystems, such as Partners in Amphibian and Reptile Conservation (PARC).

Popular pandas
Many campaigners believe that too much focus is given to protecting large mammals rather than whole ecosystems.

The developing world

Some people argue that the cost of conserving all of the world's animal species is greater than the benefits humans get from animals. The world's population is growing all the time and competition for land and resources is intense. This is especially true in **developing countries**, where people are trying to lift themselves out of extreme poverty.

Farming in Africa
Many of the world's people rely on what they can farm themselves. They know the importance of maintaining their natural surroundings.

RICH VERSUS POOR?

Many of the threats to biodiversity will be felt most in the developing world, including the effects of climate change. Some developing countries have come up with new ideas to help preserve ecosystems. In Costa Rica, landowners receive payments to conserve the rainforest land they own. The money for these payments comes from taxes on fuel and by charging businesses for the water they use. Many people argue that the whole world benefits from these ecosystems, so richer countries should pay more to protect them.

Breaking through

Rwanda is one of the 20 poorest countries in the entire world. The Rwanda Environment Management Authority has found a way to balance conservation with the needs of the country's people. By protecting the country's mountain gorillas and restoring other habitats, Rwanda has benefited from a big increase in tourism. This brings visitors and money into the country.

Rainforest protection
Encouraging rainforest-dwellers to continue to protect their ecosystems could have a bigger impact than any international agreement.

A MORAL ISSUE

Even if we ignore the importance of biodiversity to our own way of life, conservationists and scientists argue that humans have a moral responsibility to care for the other species on our planet. Just because we destroy ecosystems and change the planet for our own needs, it does not mean that we should ignore the needs and survival of the animals with which we share the planet.

Chapter five: Into the future

The fight to protect animal species is getting tougher as climate change and other human-made problems threaten the animal kingdom. However, science is battling hard to protect Earth's animal species. Scientists are discovering new solutions and technologies all the time. So what does the future hold in the battle against animal extinction?

TRACKING SPECIES

Scientists find new species all the time. Although this can be difficult in places such as dense rainforests, genetic technology means that in the future scientists will be able to track some species without actually seeing them. For example, leeches suck blood from mammals. Scientists can examine the DNA of the blood inside leeches and track the mammal species from which the blood came.

Remote-sensing technology has enabled scientists to map the plant species in a rainforest from an aircraft flying above the area. In the future this technology could be used to track animal species around the world very quickly and accurately.

Whale recovery
In 1986, commercial whaling was banned around the world. Many whale species that were close to extinction have now started to recover.

COUNTERING CLIMATE CHANGE

Future technologies are being developed to deal with the threats to animals, including the build-up of carbon dioxide in the atmosphere and oceans that is causing climate change. Renewable forms of energy, such as solar and wave power, may one day replace fossil fuels for generating electricity and powering vehicles. Although this will not stop global warming immediately, it may slow the pace of animal extinction. Yet in the future, humans and animals will still need to adapt to hotter and drier climates as a result of global warming.

Breaking through

Can science help to artificially recreate habitats that are being lost? Coral reefs are naturally built up from the hard exteriors of tiny living things. Scientists can create artificial "biorocks" underwater that support these living things. This is one of the methods we can use to help restore coral reefs.

Wilderness under threat

Can wilderness areas be protected from the search for resources such as oil and minerals?

Genes and cloning

The science of genetics is a major weapon in the ongoing battle to save Earth's animals from extinction. Each individual animal or plant has its own genes. This genetic material is inherited from its parents and determines the animal's appearance and characteristics. All animals in a species share many genes. Scientists can combine genes to change the way living things behave and even to create new animals using a process called **cloning**.

Gene genius
Scientists' understanding of genetics is improving all the time, but cloning is too complex to help preserve most species under threat.

BANKING GENES

Genetic modification of plants is common, although many people oppose it, saying that its impact on other organisms and ecosystems is not fully understood. Gene banks hold seeds of different plant species and variations within species. This means that species can be modified and, if they do become extinct, their genetic material is preserved. Could this clever technology be a way of protecting many animal species, too?

BENEFITS AND DANGERS

Scientists can already create cloned animals, although the process is very difficult and expensive. Some people believe that cloning could even help to revive animal species on the brink of extinction, but it is unlikely to be a solution for the huge number of species currently in danger. Many experts also believe that introducing cloned animals could have negative effects on species and should only be used as a last resort.

Essential insects
Scientists have not even named many of the insect species on Earth. Protecting them with genetics presents huge challenges.

Winning or losing?
The new technologies that could help to conserve animal species may also be matched by new threats that have not yet become a focus for conservation. Scientists are finding more and more tiny pieces of plastic in the oceans. We do not yet know what impact this form of pollution will have on sea creatures.

The fight continues:
Is science winning?

Future technologies, such as cloning, can never offer a complete solution to mass extinction. Even if scientists can create clones, these creatures would be unable to survive habitat loss or the other threats that drove them to extinction in the first place. If we are to preserve the awe-inspiring variety of life on Earth, we need to tackle the main causes of animal extinction. Can science protect the planet's animals and win the battle against threats to biodiversity?

Birds on the move
Habitat loss and climate change are affecting the migration (travelling) pattern of birds. Scientists are not sure how quickly birds can adapt.

Winning or losing?

The whooping crane was almost wiped out in North America because of hunting and habitat loss. When the crane was declared endangered in 1967 there were fewer than 50 left in the wild. Conservationists revived the species through habitat protection, breeding in captivity and reintroducing the birds to the wild. By 2011, there were almost 600 whooping cranes, and since then the numbers have been growing.

City life

More people are moving to live in cities all the time. Could this actually help to protect animals in wilderness areas?

MAKING PROGRESS

There are reasons to be optimistic about the progress science is making in preventing animal extinctions. People across the world understand the importance of preserving ecosystems and are trying to make this happen. Scientists are finding out more all the time about the vast numbers of animal species in our world, and discovering new technologies to protect them. There may yet be time to save many species of animals around the world if scientific advancements continue.

BATTLES YET TO COME

The question is whether these new developments will become widespread enough to make a big difference to the plight of endangered species. Unfortunately, conservation efforts can only achieve so much. The threats of climate change and other human activities are putting huge pressure on ecosystems and the intertwined lives of the animals and plants within them.

The animal story

3.5 billion years ago
The very first microscopic life appears on Earth.

65 million years ago
An enormous meteorite hits Earth in the Gulf of Mexico, contributing to the death of dinosaurs.

190,000 years ago
The first modern humans appear in Africa.

1859
Charles Darwin publishes *On the Origin of Species*, detailing the theory of evolution by natural selection.

1872
Yellowstone in the United States becomes the world's first national park.

1988
The United Nations begins to assess the progress and impact of global warming. The murder of Brazilian rainforest activist Chico Mendes brings attention to the destruction of rainforests.

1992
World leaders meet at the Earth Summit in Rio de Janeiro, Brazil, agreeing to take action to promote sustainable development.

1997
The Kyoto Protocol is agreed in Japan. Many countries agree to cuts in greenhouse gas emissions. More forests are burnt than in any other year in recorded history.

2002
Damage from coral bleaching to Australia's Great Barrier Reef is the worst on record.

2003
Protected areas around the world cover an area bigger than China and India combined.

1961
Conservation campaigning group the WWF is founded.

1962
Rachel Carson publishes *Silent Spring*, which highlights the effects of the pesticide DDT.

1972
DDT is banned in the United States.

1973
The Convention on International Trade in Endangered Species (CITES) restricts trade in animals and plants that are under threat of extinction.

1981
The Great Barrier Reef in Australia is named as one of UNESCO's World Heritage Sites.

2010
The Deepwater Horizon oil spill in the Gulf of Mexico is the world's worst accidental oil spill of all time.

2011
The destruction of Brazilian rainforest is measured at its lowest level since records began in 1980s.

The United Nations report states that oceans could be almost empty of fish by 2050. The western black rhino is declared extinct.

2014
The IUCN states that there are more than 70,000 animals on its list of threatened species.

Glossary

acidic substance that can wear away materials and damage living things

amphibian animal that spends part of its life in water and part on land, such as a frog or a toad

arthropod type of animal that has a segmented body and external skeleton, including insects and spiders

atmosphere layer of gases that surrounds Earth and contains the oxygen that humans and other animals breathe

biodiversity variety of living things in the world or in a particular ecosystem

climate change theory that Earth's climate is becoming warmer and that this is caused by human actions, such as burning fossil fuels

cloning scientific process in which an identical new organism is created from the cells of another

coral type of simple animal that has a hard outer skeleton that forms reefs

developing country country in which the economy is not yet fully developed, including many countries in Africa, Asia and South America

deoxyribonucleic acid (DNA) substance that is present in almost all living things and carries genetic information

dichlorodiphenyl-trichloroethane (DDT) pesticide used on farm crops to kill mosquitoes

ecosystem the environment and the animals and plants that live in it

evolution way that living things change over many generations to become better suited to their environment

extinct when something has completely died out

food chain chain of predators and prey that depend on each other for food

fossil fuel energy source that includes coal, oil and natural gas that has formed from the decayed remains of living things

genes chain of molecules that describes a particular characteristic of a living thing, usually made from DNA

habitat place where animals and plants live

mammal animal that provides milk for its young, including humans, dogs, bears and whales

meteorite piece of rock or metal that has fallen from space to Earth's surface

naturalist scientist who studies the natural world

pesticide chemical that is sprayed on crops to kill insects and other pests that attack them

pollinate to carry pollen from one plant to another so that the plants can reproduce

pollution harmful substances released into the land, water or the air

predator animal that hunts and eats other animals

reptile class of cold-blooded scaly mammals, including snakes and crocodiles

species group of animals that often look similar and can breed together in the wild to create offspring

tropical occurring in areas of the world found near the equator. The equator is an imaginary line around the middle of the planet.

Find out more

BOOKS

Amazon (Eyewitness), Tom Jackson
(Dorling Kindersley, 2015)

Endangered Animals (Eyewitness), Ben Hoare
(Dorling Kindersley, 2010)

*The Big Countdown: Ten Thousand, Eight Hundred
and Twenty Endangered Species in the Animal Kingdom,*
Paul Rockett (Franklin Watts, 2014)

The Future of Life on Earth (The Web of Life), Michael Bright
(Raintree, 2012)

WEBSITES

Browse this website for fabulous wildlife photos and films:
www.arkive.org

Watch this fascinating film clip about a South American
rainforest and the endangered animals that live there:
www.bbc.co.uk/education/clips/zgcnyrd

Find out about the work of WWF to save animals from extinction:
www.worldwildlife.org

Index